EMOTIONAL CONTINUITY

How Children Build Emotional Stability Through Trust, Attention, and Safe Transitions

By Tiber Knoxx

Dedication

For Young Tiber,

Who unknowingly helped reveal how emotional stability is often built quietly through trust, patience, repair, and safe transitions.

And for the parents, caregivers, educators, and emotionally exhausted humans who leave small pieces of themselves behind in every child they help guide, stabilize, protect, and believe in.

Much of what holds people together later in life may begin with the emotional continuity someone gave them long before they were old enough to understand it.

Contents

Foundational Observation

Theoretical idea: young Tiber behaves differently with me than he does with his mother or anyone else. That is normal. Children continuously test and evaluate the stability of their environment.

When I communicate with young Tiber, I remain fully engaged with him until the emotional or instructional feedback loop is completed.

One important observation is that every day is different. Attention, emotional regulation, curiosity, fatigue, and responsiveness fluctuate depending on the conditions of that particular day.

Because of this, engagement must remain adaptive rather than rigid.

For example, before beginning an activity such as counting, word puzzles, or building exercises, I first evaluate Tiber's attention span and responsiveness in real time. If his average engagement window appears short on a given day, the instructions are compressed into smaller, manageable pieces.

Instead of long explanations, communication is delivered in short bursts designed to fit within the amount of time his attention remains fully connected and emotionally engaged.

If the average engagement window appears to be approximately three seconds, the instructional input may be reduced to two-second segments in order to allow enough time for processing, response, and completion of the emotional or cognitive loop before disengagement occurs.

The objective is not forcing prolonged attention artificially. The objective is to complete small, successful loops consistently.

When the loop completes successfully, Little T often voluntarily extends his engagement window slightly longer during the next interaction instead of immediately disengaging or turning away.

Over time, this appears to gradually strengthen focus,

participation, emotional regulation, and willingness to remain engaged during increasingly complex tasks.

The important observation is that engagement continuity appears easier to maintain when communication adapts to the child's real-time processing capacity rather than forcing the child to adapt abruptly to adult pacing.

With other people, the engagement loop is frequently interrupted or distorted during moments of emotional stress. The continuity between child and caregiver breaks before the emotional process fully stabilizes.

If engagement continuity is interrupted during distress, even briefly, the emotional signal may destabilize, and the child may experience emotional fragmentation rather than emotional completion.

Young Tiber did not want to stay at daycare. He tightened his grip around my neck and attempted to suppress tears. I recognized the beginning stages of emotional destabilization.

Instead of abruptly separating from him, I created a controlled emotional transition. I maintained eye contact, verbal continuity, calm pacing, and emotional engagement. I explained that he had two choices, but that either choice would still lead to him staying safely and having a good day.

I counted down slowly while maintaining engagement continuity.

He made a choice. The right choice.

Once the emotional transition stabilized, I set him down. The reason he was being carried in the first place was due to unusually heavy tricycle traffic and what appeared to be a small logistical breakdown that had created a bottleneck along the playground concrete walkway, a place where, apparently, all traffic laws immediately collapse once tiny humans gain access to mobile equipment.

Navigating through the chaos to reach his assigned teacher occasionally felt less like entering a daycare and more like crossing an active industrial zone operated by highly emotional miniature supervisors with limited regard for pedestrian right-of-way.

Somehow, we survived the crossing. More importantly, so did the emotional transition.

When hesitation returned after separation, the teacher immediately stabilized the transition by giving him a role and responsibility, offering him the opportunity to become her assistant for the day. A short pause, a process, and then regulation returned.

He emotionally reorganized almost immediately and continued walking.

The theory is that emotional stability may depend heavily on uninterrupted emotional continuity during moments of stress and transition.

Abrupt separation may distort emotional processing by interrupting stabilization loops before completion. Repeated destabilized transitions may gradually contribute to anxiety, distrust, or emotional fragility.

The core idea is not that stress itself is harmful, but that emotional instability without continuity may become psychologically disorganizing.

Refined Introduction

Most people think childhood development happens through major events such as learning to speak, learning to walk, or the first day of school. But many of the structures that shape emotional stability are built much more quietly during transitions between certainty and uncertainty, comfort and discomfort, connection and separation.

Children are not only learning language and behavior. They are also learning whether the world feels emotionally stable. They are learning whether stress can be survived safely, whether discomfort leads to abandonment or reassurance, and whether emotional instability resolves calmly or collapses into fear.

This book began with a simple observation involving a young child resisting separation at daycare. The child was not yet in full emotional collapse, but the early signs of destabilization were already present through hesitation, tightening grip, and emotional fragility.

One approach forced separation abruptly. Another maintained emotional continuity long enough for the child to reorganize emotionally before separation occurred.

The difference was not discipline. The difference was regulation.

This book explores the possibility that emotional development may depend heavily on continuity of engagement, trust, pacing, responsiveness, and emotional safety during moments of stress and transition.

Children may not need perfect environments. They may need emotionally stable transitions.

Chapter 1

Co-Regulation and the Borrowed Nervous System

Long before children can regulate themselves emotionally, they regulate through others. This process is known as co-regulation. Co-regulation refers to the way children stabilize emotionally through the presence, responsiveness, tone, pacing, and emotional consistency of trusted adults.

The phrase borrowed nervous system is used here as a plain-language metaphor. It does not mean a child literally uses another person's nervous system. It means that a caregiver's tone, presence, rhythm, responsiveness, and emotional steadiness can help organize a child's emotional state during stress, uncertainty, or transition.

Long before children regulate themselves consistently, they regulate through relationships. A calm caregiver does more than comfort a child emotionally. The caregiver becomes part of the child's regulatory environment. Tone, eye contact, facial expression, physical presence, pacing, predictable response, and emotional repair all become signals that help the child understand whether a situation is safe, dangerous, confusing, or manageable.

This is the foundation of co-regulation. The child is not simply being comforted. The child is learning, through repeated relational experience, how distress can move back toward safety. Over time, repeated experiences of safe emotional recovery may help build the child's internal capacity for self-regulation.

In the language of Emotional Continuity, the adult temporarily helps hold the child's emotional state until the child can begin learning how to hold it internally.

John Bowlby's attachment theory provides one of the foundational structures behind this idea. Bowlby described the caregiver as a secure base from which children can explore the world. For Emotional Continuity, his work supports the idea that children do not become confident through forced independence. They become confident when the connection feels stable enough to survive distance, frustration, fear, and return.

Mary Ainsworth expanded Bowlby's work through the Strange Situation procedure, observing how young children responded to separation and reunion with caregivers in an unfamiliar setting. The relevance is direct: the child is not only learning that adults leave. The child is learning whether the connection returns safely.

Allan Schore's work connects attachment relationships to affect regulation and early brain development. His work supports the idea that emotional regulation is not built in isolation. It develops through repeated relational experiences of attunement, misattunement, and repair.

Daniel Siegel's interpersonal neurobiology provides a bridge between relationships, the mind, and the developing brain. His work emphasizes that human development is shaped through relational experience and integration. In simple terms, relationships help organize the mind.

Stephen Porges' Polyvagal Theory offers useful language for understanding how the body responds to cues of safety and threat. This framework should be used carefully and humbly, but it helps explain why tone, facial expression, proximity, rhythm, and calm presence can matter so much during distress.

Edward Tronick's Still-Face Experiment is one of the clearest demonstrations of how deeply infants depend on emotional responsiveness. In the experiment, a caregiver first interacts normally with the infant, then suddenly becomes still, emotionally flat, and unresponsive. Infants typically attempt to re-engage and often become visibly distressed when the connection is not restored.

Together, these lines of research support a simple observation: children do not regulate in isolation. They learn emotional stability through repeated experiences of safe, responsive, and repair-capable connection.

Children often borrow emotional stability from adults before they can regulate independently. Tone, eye contact, pacing, predictability, and emotional consistency become stabilizing mechanisms. Emotional interruption may therefore become psychologically significant during moments of distress and transition.

One of the clearest examples can be observed when an infant crawls, slips unexpectedly, and briefly pauses without immediately crying or reacting emotionally.

In many cases, the infant first looks toward the caregiver.

This moment is important.

The child is not only reacting to the physical event itself. The child is also searching for emotional orientation from a trusted source.

If the caregiver reacts with visible panic, fear, or alarm, the infant often begins reacting with distress shortly afterward.

But if the caregiver remains calm, emotionally stable, and reassuring, the infant frequently reorganizes emotionally and continues exploring with minimal disruption.

The event itself remained the same.

What changed was the emotional interpretation surrounding the event.

This process is sometimes referred to as social referencing, where children look toward trusted adults to help determine how situations should be emotionally understood and responded to.

Before children fully regulate internally, they often rely heavily on the emotional stability of the people around them to help organize their own reactions to uncertainty, discomfort, and stress.

Chapter 2
Emotional Continuity

Children do not experience emotional events the way adults do. Adults often focus on whether the child eventually calmed down, but emotionally, the process itself matters. Emotional continuity refers to uninterrupted emotional guidance that helps a child move from distress toward regulation safely.

This continuity may include calm pacing, emotional responsiveness, verbal reassurance, maintained engagement, and predictable transitions. The objective is not preventing all discomfort, but preventing emotional abandonment during discomfort. Children often tolerate difficult transitions surprisingly well when emotional connection remains intact throughout the process.

Chapter 3

The Architecture of Separation Anxiety

Separation anxiety may represent instability in emotional prediction rather than irrational dependency. The child does not yet fully trust whether the emotional connection remains stable during absence. The nervous system responds to uncertainty accordingly.

Children are not simply learning that adults leave. They are learning whether the connection survives separation. Transition rituals, emotional predictability, consistent return patterns, and calm separations all contribute to emotional confidence over time.

Chapter 4

Emotional Rupture and Repair

No caregiver maintains perfect emotional continuity. Every relationship experiences rupture. The critical factor is repair. Repair teaches children that discomfort does not destroy connection.

Emotionally healthy systems are not rupture-free. They are repairable.

Apology, reconnection, calm explanation, and post-conflict stabilization help children learn that relationships can survive emotional stress safely.

A simple example can be observed during the highly sensitive and politically unstable morning event known as toothbrushing.

Occasionally, before leaving the house, Little T decides that today will officially become a "no brush day."

At that point, negotiations begin.

Every possible argument is introduced:

- exhaustion
- inconvenience
- sudden philosophical opposition to toothpaste
- dissatisfaction with flavor selection
- deep concern regarding toothbrush ownership rights
- and occasionally what appears to be a complete emotional collapse over which cartoon character currently holds the highest toothpaste tube approval ratings

Unfortunately for Little T, morning schedules continue to exist regardless of emotional protest.

And if I happen to be the responsible adult assigned to managing the operation that day, the timeline generally remains non-negotiable.

Predictably, frustration eventually appears on both sides.

Voices occasionally become louder than intended.

Patience temporarily weakens. The emotional atmosphere becomes strained.

Eventually, however, the teeth are brushed.

But the important part comes afterward.

Once emotional intensity decreases, Little T often immediately begins attempting to restore emotional connection by discussing what happened, reconnecting emotionally, and exploring ways to prevent future "toothpaste-related diplomatic incidents."

The repair process itself is usually initiated by me because I understand how unreasonable and almost villainous I must occasionally appear to a small child for not maintaining a magical drawer filled with unlimited flavors of children's toothpaste instantly available at all times.

The conflict itself is not the most important part.

The restoration process is.

Children gradually learn emotional safety not

because conflict never occurs, but because emotional connection consistently returns after the conflict ends.

Chapter 5

The Language of Emotional Safety

Children often understand emotional tone before language itself. Facial expression, pacing, tension, hesitation, and calmness may communicate more powerfully than words.

Ever since I began spending more time with Little T, I have started noticing how quickly children adapt to different emotional environments and expectations.

One example appears after vacations or extended breaks from routine.

When Little T returns from vacation, I can often immediately notice small behavioral shifts:

- increased emotional intensity
- reduced patience
- attempts to emotionally negotiate outcomes through frustration
- temporary loss of structure or manners

- and occasional dramatic protests regarding highly important matters, such as being told "no" by civilization itself

Vacations temporarily change the emotional atmosphere surrounding children. Rules soften, routines loosen, schedules shift, and emotional pacing changes. Children adapt to those conditions remarkably fast.

What Little T occasionally forgets after returning home is that I do not respond strongly to emotional escalation itself.

I do not speak the language of screaming, uncontrolled howling, airborne projectiles, or emotional negotiations conducted through bubbles generated from tiny nostrils.

Instead, I usually remain calm and wait for the correct emotional opening to communicate clearly.

That timing matters.

If the emotional window is missed, the nervous

system may remain overloaded for several additional minutes. But when the communication loop reconnects successfully, the emotional atmosphere often begins regulating itself surprisingly quickly.

The words matter less than the emotional stability surrounding them.

Children continuously study emotional environments long before fully understanding language itself.

The emotional atmosphere surrounding a child quietly becomes part of the child's internal emotional structure. Over time, children gradually build assumptions about:

- conflict
- safety
- trust
- emotional availability
- and emotional recovery

through repeated emotional exposure.

Chapter 6

Stress Without Stability

Stress itself is not automatically harmful. Children require manageable stress to develop resilience. However, unmanaged stress without stabilization can become psychologically disorganizing.

A simple example can appear during ordinary instructions.

For example, asking Tiber to clean up a puzzle without giving clear or structured guidance may quickly create visible frustration.

If he does not fully understand whether the puzzle should remain assembled or be taken apart, where the box is located, or when the task is expected to be completed, uncertainty itself may begin creating emotional tension.

The task itself is small.

But the instability surrounding the task gradually

becomes larger than the task itself.

Children often attempt to resolve uncertainty through exploration. In Tiber's case, a simple instruction can unexpectedly evolve into a full-scale adventure.

If the puzzle box is not immediately visible, the task may transform into a highly important search operation across the house involving investigation, movement, experimentation, and once found, a personal assessment of whether the puzzle can fit into the box assembled or whether it must first be taken apart.

From the child's perspective, this progression often feels perfectly logical.

The original objective did not disappear.

The objective simply expanded into exploration.

Children are naturally imaginative, curious, and highly responsive to open-ended conditions. Without clear boundaries, tasks can unintentionally branch into multiple competing possibilities, many of which are significantly more exciting than the original instruction itself.

What appears externally as a distraction or refusal may sometimes be unresolved uncertainty combined with exploratory curiosity operating simultaneously.

Now compare that to a more structured transition.

Instead of simply saying, “Put the puzzle away,” the instruction becomes clearer and emotionally easier to organize internally:

“Let’s reset the puzzle first.” “Take the pieces apart and place them in the box.” “The box is on the floor next to the Hot Wheels track.” “Let’s do it now before we start the next activity.”

The task itself remains almost identical.

What changes is:

- predictability
- sequencing
- clarity
- emotional certainty

Once the expectations become visible and organized, frustration often decreases significantly.

This suggests that children may not react only to difficulty itself.

They may also react to unresolved uncertainty surrounding the process required to complete the task safely and successfully.

The issue is often not intensity alone, but instability without orientation.

Over time, chronic unpredictability, emotional withdrawal, overstimulation, and inconsistent caregiving may gradually shape emotional fragility by teaching the nervous system to expect instability instead of resolution.

Chapter 7

Why Some Children Adapt Faster Than Others

Children differ significantly in emotional sensitivity and adaptability.

Some recover rapidly from stress while others internalize instability more deeply. Temperament, attachment variation, emotional sensitivity, and environmental buffering all influence emotional resilience.

A useful example can be observed during ordinary childhood accidents and mistakes.

For example, Little T may occasionally flip over a tricycle while turning too quickly in the playground. In the moment, the emotional reaction may appear dramatic and immediate, especially if the event feels sudden, painful, or unpredictable.

But recovery speed often varies depending on

previous emotional experiences.

A child who has already encountered smaller, manageable mistakes, such as briefly missing a step on the slide ladder, stumbling while running, or becoming temporarily frustrated during play, may gradually develop stronger emotional recovery patterns when those moments are consistently stabilized by a trusted caregiver.

If the caregiver responds calmly, provides orientation, reassures the child, and helps guide the situation toward emotional resolution, the child slowly begins learning something important:

Unexpected outcomes can be worked through safely.

Over time, repeated experiences of manageable stress followed by stabilization may help children recover more efficiently from future emotional disruptions.

This does not eliminate distress.

It builds familiarity with recovery.

The same emotional event may therefore affect different children differently depending on:

- temperament
- previous experiences
- emotional sensitivity
- environmental stability
- and the consistency of emotional support surrounding stressful moments

Which is why emotional continuity must remain adaptive rather than rigid.

Children do not all regulate the same way, at the same speed, or under the same conditions.

After all, they're just like us — but tiny.

Chapter 8

The Adult Nervous System

Children regulate within systems, not isolation. Adult emotional stability, therefore, matters profoundly. An emotionally exhausted, overwhelmed, or fragmented adult may unintentionally transfer instability into everyday interactions and transitions.

A common example can be seen in parents who work long hours under continuous stress. By the time they return home, their emotional reserves may already be heavily depleted.

The parent may still deeply love the child and fully intend to remain patient, emotionally available, and engaged. However, exhaustion can quietly reduce:

- attention
- responsiveness
- emotional pacing
- frustration tolerance

- and the ability to process multiple demands simultaneously

A child's request for help, reassurance, attention, or engagement may then collide with an already overwhelmed nervous system inside an environment where small misunderstandings begin appearing more easily.

Instructions become rushed. Responses become shorter. Emotional cues are missed unintentionally.

The child, meanwhile, often does not understand the larger external pressures affecting the caregiver. The child only experiences the emotional instability occurring in the moment.

As tension increases, both the child and caregiver may begin reacting to each other's stress simultaneously, creating a feedback cycle in which emotional instability escalates on both sides.

The environment itself gradually becomes emotionally strained.

This does not necessarily happen because either person lacks care or love.

Sometimes the surrounding conditions themselves have become unstable.

Protecting the dignity of the caregiver is important because emotionally stable caregiving does not occur in ideal conditions. It often happens due to exhaustion.

Caregivers are still expected to regulate, respond, stabilize, reassure, guide, protect, explain, redirect, and remain emotionally available while simultaneously functioning on limited sleep, reduced recovery, constant interruption, and continuous physical and emotional demands.

In practical terms, this can occasionally create the strange experience of becoming what feels less like a parent and more like a multipurpose emotional support structure operating under extremely questionable labor conditions.

At various points throughout the day, the caregiver may become:

- a tissue for unexpected nose-related emergencies
- a moving napkin for pizza sauce
- a climbing structure
- a wrestling opponent
- a transportation system
- a pillow
- a snack retrieval specialist
- and occasionally what appears to be an emotionally durable pack animal expected to continue operating indefinitely regardless of structural fatigue

Oddly enough, many of these behaviors emerge not from emotional distance but from emotional safety.

Children, much like adults, often reserve their least filtered behavior for the people they trust most.

To the child, the caregiver may appear emotionally

permanent, physically indestructible, and endlessly available. The child is not consciously attempting to dehumanize the caregiver.

Instead, the child is often expressing what may be the purest form of assumed safety possible: the belief that the caregiver will remain stable even while being climbed on, coughed on, emotionally negotiated with, and occasionally treated like emotionally indestructible public infrastructure.

This does not make caregiving easy.

But it does help explain why emotionally exhausted caregivers should not automatically be interpreted as uncaring or emotionally absent.

Sometimes the surrounding demands placed on the nervous system have simply exceeded the available recovery capacity.

Children often absorb emotional environments long before consciously understanding them. Caregiver regulation, therefore, becomes part of the child's emotional architecture.

This means children are not only shaped by what adults say.

They are also shaped by:

- pacing
- emotional consistency
- tone
- recovery patterns
- tension
- patience
- and the emotional atmosphere surrounding ordinary daily life

Long before children consciously understand stress, they often learn how stress feels.

Chapter 9

Trust Before Memory

Many emotional patterns form before autobiographical memory fully develops. Children may not consciously remember early experiences, but the nervous system still adapts to repeated emotional conditions.

A simple example can be observed when a child is calmly playing near the shoreline, and an unexpected wave suddenly crashes nearby, causing the child to stumble, lose balance, and become emotionally overwhelmed before fully understanding what happened.

The emotional reaction may appear immediate and intense.

Not necessarily because the child consciously believes the environment is dangerous, but because the experience arrived faster than the child's ability to emotionally organize and process it safely in the moment.

The nervous system reacts first.

Understanding often comes later.

Even if the child does not consciously remember the specific event over time, the body may still retain traces of emotional caution, heightened alertness, or discomfort surrounding similar environments afterward.

This does not mean the child is permanently traumatized by the experience.

It means the nervous system learned that unpredictability and emotional instability were once associated with that environment.

Early emotional learning often develops this way: through repeated emotional experiences occurring long before the child can consciously explain or fully remember them.

Long before detailed memory forms, emotional assumptions about safety, trust, separation, and regulation begin developing internally.

Chapter 10

Safe Enough to Separate

The goal of emotional continuity is not dependency. It is confidence. Securely attached children often separate more confidently because they expect emotional stability even during absence.

Healthy emotional systems do not eliminate separation. They make separation survivable through predictable trust, stable connection, and emotional reassurance.

And for now, Young T will continue enjoying the wonderfully chaotic system in which he and his tiny human friends ride tricycles as though traffic laws simply do not apply to emotionally stable little bundles of joy on wheels.

Apparently, emotionally stable children explore more freely.

Case Study: When the Signal Changed

One morning during daycare drop-off, young Tiber, like many children entering a new environment, did not want to stay.

He cried as I prepared to leave.

At first, nothing about the situation appeared unusual. Separation distress is a normal part of childhood development, particularly when a child is transitioning between attachment figures and unfamiliar environments.

As I stepped back to leave, his crying continued.

A teacher approached and attempted to engage him. The interaction lasted approximately two minutes. Throughout this period, the tone and rhythm of his crying remained largely unchanged. He was upset, but the emotional signal appeared stable.

Then something changed.

The teacher looked at him and said:

“You have boogers. We should go find you a tissue.”

Rather than making immediate corrections the teacher simply stated an obvious fact.

Immediately after this statement, the sound of his crying changed.

The pitch increased.

The rhythm changed.

The emotional quality of the signal changed.

It was not simply louder crying.

It felt different.

The change was so abrupt that I instinctively reacted. I walked back, wiped his nose with my hand, and cleaned my hand on my pants. In that moment, there was no difference between doing that and becoming a walking tissue for Tiber. The objective hadn't changed, only the interpretation of the situation had. My attention remained on preserving his comfort, not on finding the most sanitary solution.

The reaction was immediate and largely automatic.

At that moment, I had the impression that he was no longer communicating separation distress alone. The signal felt closer to a request for protection.

Whether that interpretation was objectively correct is less important than the observation itself.

The condition changed.

The signal changed.

That sequence is what makes the event meaningful.

From an Emotional Continuity perspective, children are not only responding to events. They are responding to how those events are experienced. Two adults can observe the same interaction and reach different conclusions about what occurred, but the child's nervous system still processes the experience in real time.

A child who is crying because a caregiver is leaving is experiencing one condition.

A child who suddenly feels exposed, embarrassed, misunderstood, or unsupported may be experiencing an entirely different condition.

The distinction matters.

The emotional signal may look similar to an outside observer, but the underlying cause can be fundamentally different.

What happened next made the observation even more interesting.

After I wiped Little Tiber's nose, the teacher commented:

"They're egocentric at that age."

The statement itself was not what captured my attention, What captured my attention was the framework behind it.

For a moment, I found myself asking a question that had little to do with tissues, crying, or developmental terminology.

Who exactly is responsible for interpreting the emotional lives of children?

The teacher's statement may have been technically correct. Developmental psychology has long recognized that young children often struggle to fully understand perspectives outside of their own. In that sense, describing a child as egocentric is neither unusual nor necessarily inaccurate.

But accuracy and understanding are not always the same thing.

The moment caused me to wonder whether I was observing a developing mind or a managed behavior.

Was the statement intended to explain the child's experience?

Or was it intended to dismiss it?

I could not know.

Yet the question remained.

In childcare environments, adults are often

responsible for large groups of children. Systems must function. Procedures must be followed. Schedules must be maintained. From an operational standpoint, this makes perfect sense.

However, children are not merely participants in a system, they are minds in development.

Every interaction contributes to the construction of trust, expectation, emotional regulation, and self-perception.

This raises a more difficult question:

Is qualification measured by the ability to manage children, or by the ability to understand them?

The two are not always identical.

For example, a person can be highly qualified to supervise a classroom. The same person can be highly qualified to maintain order and equally qualified to execute policy. Yet that same person can still miss subtle changes occurring within a child's emotional world.

The distinction matters.

While preparing this manuscript, I asked an important person in my life to read this chapter before publication. She serves as the director of an early childhood education center, overseeing a system responsible for the care and development of some of the most fragile and adaptive systems known to us—young children. Every day, she directs a system operating within larger systems: children, families, educators, regulations, and community expectations.

Her feedback was thoughtful, candid, and invaluable. She challenged my assumptions where appropriate, reinforced ideas that reflected the realities of caring for children, and ultimately encouraged me to keep this chapter as part of the book.

Her name and place of work remain private at my request and with my respect for her privacy. What matters is not who she is, but what her perspective represents: that meaningful dialogue between different ways of understanding children strengthens both the ideas in this book and the systems entrusted with their care.

A child who is safe is not necessarily secure.

A child who is compliant is not necessarily understood.

A child who is quiet is not necessarily stable.

The challenge of emotional continuity is that many of the signals that matter most are invisible to systems designed primarily to manage behavior.

This moment raises an important question:

How often do adults focus on solving the visible problem while missing the condition producing the emotional signal?

The tissue itself was not the issue.

The boogers were not the issue.

The observable event was trivial.

What mattered was the possibility that the child's

internal experience changed.

The lesson is not that the teacher was wrong.

The lesson is that emotional signals often contain information beyond the behavior being observed.

Children rarely possess the vocabulary necessary to explain these changes.

Instead, they communicate through shifts in tone, rhythm, posture, expression, and emotional intensity.

The signal changed.

The question for caregivers is whether we notice when it does.

Because emotional continuity often depends on recognizing those transitions before they become fragmentation.

The purpose of this observation is not to criticize a teacher, a daycare, or a profession.

It is to highlight a question that deserves attention:

How often do we evaluate childcare based on visible

behavior while overlooking the invisible development occurring beneath it?

The answer may determine whether children learn merely to function within systems or learn to trust the people guiding them through those systems.

Unmanaged Load Accumulation

One of the most common misconceptions about stability is the belief that strong people carry more weight than everyone else.

At first glance, this appears true.

Some individuals seem capable of handling enormous responsibility. They absorb stress, solve problems, support others, and continue functioning long after most people would have reached their limit.

Because they remain standing, observers often conclude that they are stable.

This conclusion may be incorrect.

The ability to carry load is not the same as the ability to manage load.

A bridge does not remain standing because it ignores weight.

A bridge remains standing because weight is

distributed.

The same principle applies to people.

Many forms of emotional fragmentation do not begin with weakness; they begin with accumulation.

Responsibilities accumulate.

Decisions accumulate.

Unfinished conversations accumulate.

Unresolved conflicts accumulate.

Expectations accumulate.

Over time, the individual may continue functioning while the hidden load grows larger, while from the outside, nothing appears wrong, because the person still goes to work, fulfills obligations and still appears reliable.

Yet beneath the surface, capacity is slowly being consumed.

The danger is not the presence of load.

The danger is the absence of release.

Most systems are designed with some form of pressure management. For example, industrial facilities have relief valves, electrical systems have breakers, aircraft have redundancy, and organizations have delegation structures.

Healthy systems assume that load will eventually exceed normal operating conditions and prepare accordingly.

We human beings often do the opposite; we treat endurance as a virtue and release as a weakness.

As a result, we become exceptionally skilled at carrying load and remarkably poor at managing it.

The outcome is predictable.

What is not released accumulates, what accumulates eventually alters behavior, what alters behavior eventually alters relationships, and what alters relationships eventually threatens continuity.

This process is rarely dramatic since it often appears as impatience. emotional distance, reduced availability, difficulty concentrating, loss of curiosity. withdrawal, irritability.

The person may not even recognize the source of the change.

They only experience the symptoms while the hidden condition remains invisible.

From an Emotional Continuity perspective, stability is not determined by how much load a person can carry.

Stability is determined by how effectively load is distributed, processed, and released.

This distinction matters because many caregivers, parents, teachers, leaders, and operators are evaluated according to endurance, yet endurance alone is a poor predictor of long-term stability.

The strongest systems are not the systems that never experience pressure; they are the systems that prevent pressure from accumulating faster than it can be managed.

This raises a question rarely asked in discussions of emotional health:

How much of what we call burnout is actually unmanaged load accumulation?

The answer may explain why some individuals appear stable for years before suddenly exhibiting signs of fragmentation.

The collapse was not sudden; the accumulation was simply hidden.

Continuity is preserved not by eliminating load, but by ensuring that load never exceeds the system's ability to process it.

The goal is not endurance.

The goal is sustainable stability.

After all, the children deserve better from us.

Preserving Caregiver Capacity

Many institutions evaluate caregiver performance while giving comparatively little attention to the conditions required to preserve caregiver capacity over time.

This creates the caregiver paradox.

This creates a structural contradiction.

The emotional continuity experienced by children depends heavily on the emotional availability of adults. Yet the adults responsible for providing that stability are frequently expected to absorb increasing emotional load without comparable systems designed to preserve their own operating capacity.

Early in my career, I worked at a large integrated steel manufacturing facility. What struck me was that the operation extended far beyond furnaces, rolling mills, and production lines. The site included medical services, a cafeteria, fitness facilities, equipment stores, employee services, and other resources that, at first glance, appeared unrelated to steel production.

With time, it became clear that these systems were not peripheral; they were operational. Their purpose was to preserve the stability of the workforce by reducing unnecessary friction before it accumulated into lost capacity. A meal eliminated one problem. Medical services prevented another. Accessible equipment reduced delays. Fitness and recovery supported long-term performance. None of these systems produced steel directly, yet each preserved the people responsible for producing it.

Industrial organizations often understand a principle that is less visible in human-centered professions: sustained performance depends upon preserving the conditions that allow people to continue performing.

The same principle applies to caregiving.

Reducing unnecessary administrative burden, providing predictable opportunities for recovery, maintaining reasonable staffing flexibility, improving communication pathways, ensuring access to peer support, and making professional resources readily available all reduce cumulative load before it begins altering judgment, patience, attention, and emotional availability.

These measures are often viewed as employee benefits.

From an Emotional Continuity perspective, they are better understood as stability-preservation mechanisms.

A pressure relief valve reacts after pressure has accumulated.

A well-designed system attempts to prevent unnecessary pressure from accumulating in the first place.

That distinction is significant.

The question is not simply whether caregivers are qualified.

The more important question is whether the

environment preserves that qualification as demands increase.

Children experience the stability of the caregiver.

The caregiver experiences the stability of the system.

If the second relationship is neglected, the first eventually becomes increasingly difficult to sustain.

The strongest caregiving environments are not those that demand unlimited endurance from adults.

They are the environments that recognize emotional capacity as a finite operational resource and deliberately preserve it.

After all, emotional continuity is not produced by asking caregivers to carry more.

It is preserved by ensuring they are never required to carry more than the system was designed to support.

Final Chapter

Emotional Stability Is Built Quietly

Children constantly learn whether distress is survivable, whether connection remains stable during discomfort, and whether emotions are safe to express. Most of this learning happens quietly through repeated emotional experiences over time.

A calm goodbye, a repaired misunderstanding, a predictable return, and a trusted voice during uncertainty may become emotionally foundational experiences.

Children do not require perfect adults.

They require emotionally stable transitions that allow emotional discomfort to resolve without abandonment.

Children build emotional strength when they learn that a connection can survive discomfort safely.

Over time, repeated experiences of emotional

stability, repair, reassurance, and safe recovery may gradually strengthen the nervous system's expectation that distress can be survived without emotional collapse.

But the reverse may also be true.

If emotional continuity can reinforce safety, trust, confidence, and resilience, then repeated instability may also reinforce fear, emotional fragmentation, unpredictability, and insecurity over time.

Children continuously adapt to the emotional environments surrounding them, whether those environments are stabilizing or destabilizing.

Which is why emotional continuity matters.

Not because discomfort can be eliminated, but because emotional environments quietly shape the way human beings learn to experience stress, trust, connection, and recovery throughout life.

Perhaps the smallest moments of emotional stability matter more than we realize.

And perhaps that is how we learn to safely hold lightning in a bottle.

Understanding the Framework

Concept	Framework Application
Emotional Continuity	Maintaining stable emotional engagement long enough for the child to process stress, learning, uncertainty, or separation without emotional disorganization.
Co-Regulation	The caregiver temporarily functions as an external stabilizing system while the child's independent regulation abilities continue developing.
Emotional Orientation	During uncertainty, children often search for emotional direction from trusted adults before

	deciding how to react emotionally.
Social Referencing	Children observe the emotional response of caregivers to determine whether an event should be interpreted as safe, dangerous, stressful, or manageable.
Emotional Stability	Emotional stability develops through repeated successful experiences of distress resolving safely without abandonment or prolonged instability.
Emotional Fragmentation	Emotional overload may occur when uncertainty, unpredictability, unclear expectations, or interrupted engagement

	exceed the child's ability to organize emotionally.
Stabilization	Calm pacing, predictable guidance, emotional reassurance, and continuity help reorganize emotional distress into manageable emotional experiences.
Emotional Recovery	Recovery strengthens when children repeatedly experience that mistakes, discomfort, separation, or stress can safely resolve over time.
Emotional Transition	Smooth transitions reduce emotional shock by preserving engagement continuity during moments of separation,

	change, or uncertainty.
Separation Anxiety	Emotional distress during separation may increase when the child cannot confidently predict emotional reconnection or stability after separation occurs.
Environmental Buffering	Stable routines, emotionally calm adults, predictable responses, and reassurance reduce the destabilizing effect of stressful experiences.
Manageable Stress	Children build resilience when stress remains difficult enough to challenge them while still allowing emotional recovery and stabilization.

Emotional Prediction	Children gradually build internal expectations about whether situations, transitions, or discomfort will resolve safely or become emotionally unstable.
Emotional Safety	Emotional safety allows children to express fear, frustration, uncertainty, or vulnerability without expecting rejection or abandonment.
Rupture and Repair	Emotional relationships remain healthy not because disruptions never occur, but because emotional reconnection consistently restores stability afterward.

Emotional Atmosphere	Children continuously absorb emotional pacing, tension, patience, frustration, and emotional consistency from the surrounding environment.
Nervous System Exhaustion	Caregiver fatigue, overstimulation, and prolonged stress may reduce emotional responsiveness, patience, and stabilization capacity.
Caregiver Regulation	The caregiver's emotional state becomes part of the child's emotional environment and strongly influences emotional interpretation and recovery.
Feedback Loop	Emotional or instructional

	interactions become more stable when engagement remains active until emotional resolution or understanding is reached.
Engagement Continuity	Sustained emotional attention during stressful moments helps prevent emotional disorganization caused by abrupt interruption or emotional withdrawal.
Exploratory Expansion	Children may transform unclear instructions into imaginative exploration when task boundaries, expectations, or endpoints remain undefined.
Instability Without Orientation	Emotional stress increases when children experience

	uncertainty without sufficient explanation, structure, predictability, or emotional guidance.
Emotional Architecture	Repeated emotional experiences gradually shape the child's long-term internal expectations regarding trust, stress, safety, and emotional recovery.
Structural Fatigue	Continuous caregiving demands without sufficient recovery may gradually reduce emotional regulation capacity even in loving and highly committed caregivers.
Lightning in a Bottle	A symbolic metaphor

	describing the process of safely stabilizing emotionally volatile developmental energy through trust, emotional continuity, regulation, and safe environmental conditions over time.

References and Source Notes

Ainsworth, M. D. S., Blehar, M. C., Waters, E., & Wall, S. (1978). Patterns of Attachment: A Psychological Study of the Strange Situation. Hillsdale, NJ: Lawrence Erlbaum.

Bowlby, J. (1988). A Secure Base: Parent-Child Attachment and Healthy Human Development. Basic Books.

Cassidy, J. (2013). Contributions of Attachment Theory and Research: A Framework for Future Research, Translation, and Policy. Development and Psychopathology / PMC.

Porges, S. W. (2022). Polyvagal Theory: A Science of Safety. Frontiers in Integrative Neuroscience.

Schore, A. N. (2000/2001). Attachment and the Regulation of the Right Brain; The Effects of a Secure Attachment Relationship on Right Brain Development, Affect Regulation, and Infant Mental Health.

Siegel, D. J. (2001). Toward an Interpersonal Neurobiology of the Developing Mind. Infant Mental Health Journal.

Tronick, E. Z., and later Still-Face Paradigm research. See also Northrup & Iverson (2019), A Transactional Model of Infant Still-Face Response and Mother-Infant Affective Communication, PMC.

About The Author

Tiber Knoxx works within the operations and planning sectors of heavy civil construction, where timing, logistics, coordination, and system stability operate in environments where failure carries real consequences.

Outside of industrial operations, his work gradually expanded toward a different form of continuity: human emotional development.

What began as simple observations involving caregiving, emotional regulation, stress, trust, and child development slowly evolved into a broader continuity-centered framework exploring how emotional stability forms through repeated experiences of safety, repair, attention, pacing, and trusted connection.

Emotional Continuity emerged from those observations.

Rather than approaching emotional development strictly through abstract theory, Gonzalez focuses on the small, repeated moments that quietly shape emotional architecture over time: calm transitions, repaired misunderstandings, emotional predictability, co-regulation, and emotionally stable recovery during discomfort.

His broader framework ecosystem also includes *Conditional Reality* and *Recursive Fragility*, works exploring continuity systems, adaptive stabilization, operational drift, and the relationship between conditions and outcomes across both human and institutional environments.

At the center of the work remains a simple idea: Human beings often stabilize through continuity long before they fully understand it.

www.ingramcontent.com/pod-product-compliance
Lightning Source LLC
LaVergne TN
LVHW010738061126
851857LV00014B/1535